Framing the Problem

Framing the Problem

Causes and Consequences of a Shrinking Great Salt Lake

Kevin D. Perry

The University of Utah Press
Salt Lake City

Publication of this edition is made possible in part by The Wallace Stegner Center for Land, Resources and the Environment, S. J. Quinney College of Law and by The Tanner Trust Fund, Special Collections Department, J. Willard Marriott Library

This lecture was originally delivered on March 16, 2023, at the 28th annual symposium of the Wallace Stegner Center for Land, Resources and the Environment. The symposium is supported by the R. Harold Burton Foundation, the founding and lead donor since 1996, and by the Cultural Vision Fund and The Nature Conservancy.

The Defiance House Man colophon is a registered trademark of the University of Utah Press. It is based on a four-foot-tall Ancient Puebloan pictograph (late PIII) near Glen Canyon, Utah.

LIBRARY OF CONGRESS CATALOGING-IN-PUBLICATION DATA
Names: Perry, Kevin D., author. | University of Utah. Wallace Stegner
    Center for Land, Resources and the Environment. Annual Symposium (28th
    : 2023 : Salt Lake City, Utah)
Title: Framing the problem : causes and consequences of a shrinking Great
    Salt Lake / Kevin D. Perry.
Identifiers: LCCN 2023055124 | ISBN 9781647691622 (paperback) | ISBN
    9781647691639 (ebook)
Subjects: LCSH: Salt lake ecology--Utah--Great Salt Lake. | Climatic
    changes--Risk management--Utah--Great Salt Lake. | Dust
    control--Environmental aspects--Utah--Great Salt Lake. | Great Salt Lake
    (Utah)--Environmental conditions. | Great Salt Lake (Utah)--History.
Classification: LCC QH105.U8 P47 2024 | DDC
    577.63/90979242--dc23/eng/20231219
LC record available at https://lccn.loc.gov/2023055124

Front cover photo by Liberty Blake.
Errata and further information on this and other titles available at UofUpress.com
Printed and bound in the United States of America.

FOREWORD

The Wallace Stegner Lecture serves as a public forum for addressing the critical environmental issues that confront society. Conceived in 2009 on the centennial of Wallace Stegner's birth, the lecture honors the Pulitzer Prize–winning author, educator, and conservationist by bringing a prominent scholar, public official, advocate, or spokesperson to the University of Utah with the aim of informing and promoting public dialogue over the relationship between humankind and the natural world. The lecture is delivered in connection with the Wallace Stegner Center's annual symposium and published by the University of Utah Press to ensure broad distribution. Just as Wallace Stegner envisioned a more just and sustainable world, the lecture acknowledges Stegner's enduring conservation legacy by giving voice to "the geography of hope" that he evoked so eloquently throughout his distinguished career.

The 2023 Wallace Stegner Lecture delivered by Kevin D. Perry is titled "Framing the Problem: Causes and Consequences of a Shrinking Great Salt Lake."

Robert B. Keiter, Director
WALLACE STEGNER CENTER FOR LAND,
RESOURCES AND THE ENVIRONMENT

It is difficult to contemplate life in northern Utah without Great Salt Lake (GSL). Yet, due to a combination of unsustainable water diversion, drought, and climate change, we are forced to do just that. Whether Salt Lake City and other residents along the Wasatch Front realize it, our very existence is intertwined with the fate of our namesake. In addition to being a recreational retreat for boaters, swimmers, bird watchers, photographers, stargazers, artists, hikers, mountain bikers, rockhounds, duck hunters, and campers, the lake contributes substantially to the local economy, provides vital habitat for a myriad of species, and gives rise to our reputation for the "Greatest Snow on Earth." The lake also holds great cultural significance to the settlers who declared: "This is the place" in the mid-nineteenth century, and to the Native Americans who lived in harmony with it for millennia.

Great Salt Lake Importance

GSL is arguably the most important ecological oasis in the western United States. The saline lake and its surrounding wetlands support a biologically diverse ecosystem that serves as a critical stopover and staging area for an estimated ten million migratory birds annually. These critical habitats, which serve at least 338 bird species,[1] were designated a Western Hemisphere Shorebird Reserve Network (WHSRN) site of hemispheric importance in 1991.

GSL is also an important contributor to the economy of the state of Utah. The most significant economic impact is from the mineral extraction industry, which uses water from the lake to produce goods worth more than $1.3 billion annually.[2] Products extracted from GSL include road salt, magnesium chloride ($MgCl_2$), potassium sulfate (K_2SO_4, also known as sulfate of potash), water softener, table salt, magnesium metal, and lithium metal. GSL also supports a $67 million per year brine shrimp industry, which harvests brine shrimp cysts for use in fish and shrimp hatcheries around the world.[3] GSL is currently the world's largest single source of brine shrimp cysts, producing about 45 percent of the worldwide total (by volume).

GSL enhances the wintertime precipitation downwind of the lake, contributing 5-8 percent of the total snow water equivalent to the adjacent Wasatch Mountains.[4] Although this amount may sound negligible, lake-effect snow is most likely to occur from October through early December when the water in GSL is warm compared to the cold air outbreaks associated with the incoming storms. This early season snowfall is particularly beneficial to ski resorts as it reduces the need for costly artificial snow generation. Late season lake-effect snow can prolong the ski season by adding to the snow-pack and increasing the reflectivity of the surface, which gradually darkens due to snow grain metamorphosis, and the deposition of mineral dust and black carbon. It has been estimated that every inch of snowfall is worth $2.8 million to Utah's $1.6 billion ski tourism industry.[5]

Utahns have been visiting GSL for recreational purposes for more than 150 years. The GSL Yacht Club was established in 1877 and supported a vibrant sailing community until low water levels forced the closure of the last remaining marina and the removal of all boats in 2022. A large resort known as Saltair was constructed on the south shore of GSL in 1893 and served nearly 500,000 people annually before it was destroyed by fire in 1925.[6] Although it was rebuilt, Saltair never regained its popularity, in part due to the Great Depression, World War II, and receding lake levels, and it closed permanently in 1958. Today, the GSL ecosystem encompasses one federal wildlife area, three state parks, ten state wildlife/waterfowl management areas, and several privately held parcels that allow public access (table 1). Together, these areas offer a wealth of rec-reation opportunities including water activities, hiking/biking, artistic endeavors, wildlife viewing, hunting, and camping. Antelope Island State Park, which is located in the middle of GSL (fig. 1), is the most visited site associated with the lake, recording more than

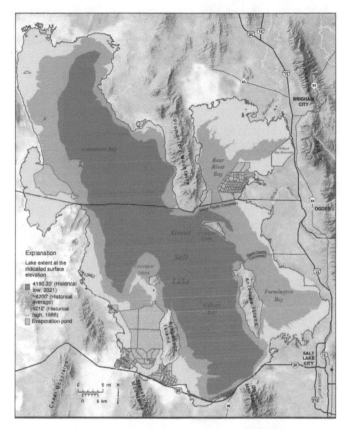

Figure 1. Areal extent and elevation of Great Salt Lake at historical high (1986), average, and near historical low-water levels (2021). [Gwynn, 1996]

one million visitors in recent years. While it is difficult to quantify the overall impact of GSL on local tourism, it is clear that the lake, its islands, and surrounding wetlands provide unique and easily accessible recreational opportunities for the more than 2.5 million residents along the Wasatch Front.

Archaeological evidence suggests that people have lived in northern Utah since shortly after the end of the last ice age. The ancient people who lived in the region were hunter-gatherers who relied on the abundant resources provided by the lake, including fish and waterfowl. Remarkably, archaeologists recently discovered

TABLE 1. SUMMARY OF RECREATION OPPORTUNITIES AT GREAT SALT LAKE

State Parks	Primary Activities
Antelope Island State Park	Biking, boating, camping, hiking, horseback riding, photography, rockhounding, stargazing, swimming, wildlife viewing
Great Salt Lake State Park	Boating, camping, hiking, photography, swimming, wildlife viewing
Willard Bay State Park	Boating, camping, fishing, photography, wildlife viewing

Federal Wildlife Areas	Primary Activities
Bear River Migratory Bird Refuge	Fishing, hunting, photography, wildlife viewing

State Wildlife/Waterfowl Management Areas	Primary Activities
Farmington Bay Waterfowl Management Area	Biking, boating, hiking, hunting, wildlife viewing
Gunnison Island State Wildlife Management Area	Wildlife viewing (by permit)
Harold S. Crane Waterfowl Management Area	Boating, hiking, hunting, wildlife viewing
Howard Slough Waterfowl Management Area	Biking, boating, hiking, hunting, wildlife viewing
Locomotive Springs Wildlife Management Area	Biking, fishing, hiking, hunting, wildlife viewing
Ogden Bay Waterfowl Management Area	Boating, hiking, hunting, wildlife viewing
Public Shooting Grounds Waterfowl Management Area	Hunting, wildlife viewing
Salt Creek Waterfowl Management Area	Boating, hunting, wildlife viewing
Timpie Springs Waterfowl Management Area	Hunting, wildlife viewing
Willard Spur Waterfowl Management Area	Boating, hunting, wildlife viewing

Privately Owned Areas of Interest	Primary Activities
George S. and Dolores Doré Eccles Wildlife Education Center	Biking, hiking, wildlife viewing
Great Salt Lake Shorelands Preserve	Hiking, wildlife viewing
Great Salt Lake Nature Reserve	Biking, hiking, wildlife viewing
Gilmore Sanctuary	Wildlife viewing (by permit)
Inland Sea Shorebird Reserve	Wildlife viewing (by permit)
Lee Creek Area	Hiking, wildlife viewing
Legacy Nature Preserve	Wildlife viewing (by permit)
The Great Saltair	Concerts, hiking, wildlife viewing

Public Areas of Interest	Primary Activities
Dolphin Island	Biking, hiking, photography, wildlife viewing
Fremont Island	Biking, hiking, photography
Rozel Point tar oil field	Hiking, photography
Spiral Jetty	Hiking, photography, swimming, stargazing
Stansbury Island (mix of public and private)	Biking, camping, hiking, photography, rockhounding, stargazing, wildlife viewing

eighty-eight human footprints preserved in the alkali flats on the current Utah Test and Training Range site that date to more than 12,000 years ago.[7] Stepping into one of the many caves surrounding GSL often reveals evidence of past habitation in the form of well-preserved pictographs (fig. 2). Artifacts from some of these caves are on permanent display at the Natural History Museum of Utah.

Over time, the various tribes that inhabited the area developed their own unique cultural traditions and languages, built communities, and formed complex societies that were well-adapted to the harsh desert environment. Modern tribes such as the Shoshone, Paiute, Goshute, and Utes continue to maintain deep cultural

Figure 2. Pictographs found in small caves on the periphery of Great Salt Lake. Photos by Kevin Perry.

connections to GSL and the surrounding area. Pioneers from the Church of Jesus Christ of Latter-day Saints arrived in what is now Salt Lake Valley in July 1847. Upon exiting Emigration Canyon and viewing the Salt Lake Valley and GSL for the first time, the leader of the group, Brigham Young, is famously quoted as saying: "This is the right place; drive on." Whether these words were actually uttered is debatable,[8] but the sentimentality and the cultural connection that were established on that day have endured.

ORIGINS OF GREAT SALT LAKE

The Great Basin is a vast watershed in the western United States; it covers parts of six states and has no outlet to the ocean. It consists of a series of isolated north-south trending mountain ranges with intervening valleys situated between the Sierra Nevada and Cascade Mountains to the west and the Rocky Mountains to the east. Elevations range from approximately 4,000 ft. in the lowest valleys to over 12,000 ft. for the highest peaks. This high-altitude desert ecosystem

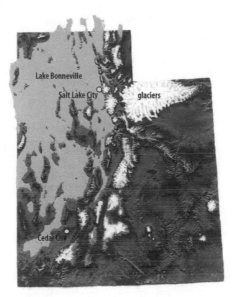

Figure 3. Map showing the maximum extent of Lake Bonneville approximately 18,000 years ago. [Utah Geological Survey]

experiences hot summers, cold winters, and a semi-arid climate. Precipitation in the Great Basin generally falls as snow in the mountains where it accumulates throughout the colder months. As the snowpack melts, it feeds streams, recharges groundwater, and eventually pools in ephemeral lakes where the water evaporates, leaving behind dried areas called playa. At the peak of the last ice age (approximately 18,000 years ago) the climate of the Great Basin was about 5°C cooler and somewhat drier than today.[9] The cooler temperatures dramatically reduced evaporation, causing the lowland lakes to grow in size until they merged, eventually forming two massive lakes within the Great Basin (Lake Lahontan in Nevada and Lake Bonneville in Utah). The larger of these two lakes, Lake Bonneville (fig. 3), reached a maximum depth of 980 ft. and covered almost 20,000 mi.[2], making it about the same size as Lake Michigan.[10]

Shortly after the last glacial maximum, Lake Bonneville filled to capacity and began overflowing Red Rock Pass in southern Idaho.[11]

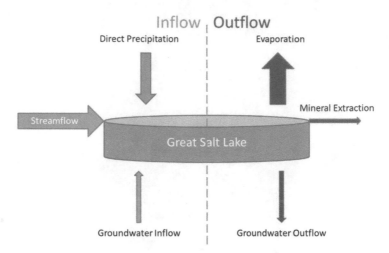

Figure 4. Diagram showing the major inflows and outflows of water to Great Salt Lake. When inflow > outflow the lake level will rise. When inflow < outflow the lake level will decrease.

The outflow from the lake quickly eroded the unconsolidated material near the pass and unleashed a torrent of water that flowed down the Marsh River Valley to the Snake River, where it eventually joined the Columbia River and flowed to the Pacific Ocean. The Bonneville Flood, which was the second largest flood in geologic history, released an estimated 1,200 cubic miles (mi.^{3}) of water within a short period of time and permanently drained more than 350 ft. of water from Lake Bonneville.[12] As the climate warmed at the end of the ice age, evaporation rates increased. Over time, Lake Bonneville gradually receded, with GSL being the largest remaining remnant. As the water evaporated, the lake transformed from a freshwater ecosystem to a saline lake.

For thousands of years, GSL has waxed and waned in response to annual and decadal precipitation patterns. As a terminal basin lake, its elevation is controlled by the relative inflow versus outflow of water. Inflow is derived from direct precipitation that falls on the lake, riverine streamflow (i.e., the Bear, Jordan, and Weber Rivers), and groundwater infiltration. Outflow in the natural lake system is dominated by evaporation, which is inextricably linked to temperature. In the modern age, anthropogenic activities such as mineral extraction have created an additional outflow pathway (fig. 4). On an annual timescale, the lake rises in the spring with the snowmelt and declines during the summer and fall due to evaporation. On decadal timescales, GSL equilibrates with the prevailing climatic conditions. When the system is in equilibrium, higher than normal amounts of precipitation will cause the elevation of the lake to temporarily increase, while lower than normal amounts of precipitation will have the opposite effect.

STATE OF THE LAKE

The elevation of GSL has been continuously monitored since 1848.[13] Although the average elevation of the lake has been 4,199 ft. above sea level over the last 125 years, it has experienced significant decadal variations (fig. 5). In the 1980s, a series of massive snow years caused the lake to rise to its contemporary record height of 4,211.6 ft. After

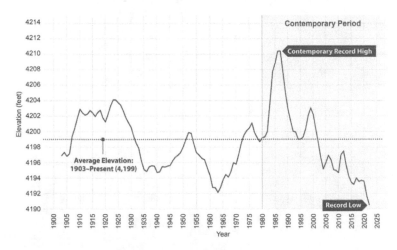

Note: 2022 annual average calculated from daily average elevation through September 23.
Sources: US Geological Survey Historical Elevation at Saltair Boat Harbor

Figure 5. Lake elevation time series measured in the southern arm of Great Salt Lake near the Saltair Boat Harbor.

Figure 6. Satellite images of Great Salt Lake from December 1984 (top) and November 2022 (bottom) showing the dramatic decrease in the surface area of the lake. [NASA]

the peak in 1986-1987, there has been a clear and sustained downward trend in lake elevation. Measurements from the last year indicated that 2022 had the lowest annual elevation in recorded history. The dramatic decrease in the lake surface area is evident in the comparison images from 1984 and 2022 (fig. 6).

The situation in 2022 became extremely dire in November, when the lake elevation dropped to 4,188.7 ft. and the salinity of the southern arm of GSL rose to more than 19 percent. During this period, Farmington Bay and Bear River Bay in the southeast and northeast quadrants of the lake were completely dry except for small river channels to the Jordan and Bear Rivers. The area of exposed lakebed now exceeds 800 square miles (mi.²). For comparison purposes, 800 mi.² is larger than the island of Maui in Hawaii and more than 50 percent the size of Rhode Island.

Why is Great Salt Lake Shrinking?

The three factors contributing to the elevation decrease of GSL include climate change, drought, and water diversion. As the climate warms, evaporation rates increase, making it more difficult to keep water in the lake. We are also amidst the worst megadrought in the last 1,200 years, which has led to paltry snowpacks over most of the last twenty years. Lastly, more than two million acre-feet (MAF) of water per year are depleted from the tributary streams and used for other purposes. Determining the relative contribution of each of these processes to declining lake elevation is a complicated endeavor. However, the GSL Strike Team, which was formed at the request of state legislators, brings together experts in public policy, hydrology, water management, climatology, and dust to provide impartial, data-informed, and solution-oriented support for Utah decision-makers. The GSL Strike Team published a Policy Assessment Report in February 2023 that summarizes the current scientific understanding of the processes leading to water loss from the GSL ecosystem.[14]

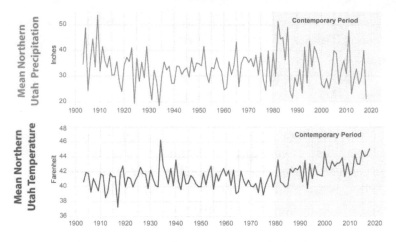

Figure 7. Time series measurements of average precipitation (top) and average temperatures (bottom) for northern Utah. [adapted from Brooks et al., 2021]

Climate Change

The data shows that there was no trend in the mean air temperatures for northern Utah over the last 125 years up to the early 1980s (fig. 7). After that, there has been a clear increase in average temperatures for the region. The experts of the GSL Strike Team determined that this temperature increase explains 8-11 percent of the water loss from GSL over the last thirty-five years. As the climate continues to warm, global precipitation will increase due to enhanced evaporation from the world's oceans.[15] However, climate models show that the increased precipitation will not be evenly distributed around the world. For example, the eastern U.S. is likely to become wetter while the western U.S. will become drier.[16] Fortunately, for northern Utah the demarcation line between increased and decreased precipitation will likely pass through central Utah. This means the GSL Watershed is expected to have a slight (13 percent) increase in precipitation over the next century. Unfortunately, the increased precipitation will be completely offset by a 17 percent increase in evaporation over the same time period. The net result is that climate change will make it slightly more difficult to retain water in GSL over the next century.

Drought

The ongoing megadrought, a severe and long-lasting drought that spans multiple decades, has also impacted GSL. It is characterized by significantly below-average precipitation, increased temperatures, and reduced snowpacks, all lasting more than twenty years. Megadroughts are somewhat rare and are typically associated with natural climate variability, such as changes in ocean circulation patterns or variations in solar radiation. Scientists have documented eight megadroughts in the western U.S. in the last 1,200 years and only two have persisted for more than thirty years. The current megadrought in the western U.S., which began in 2000,[17] is the most severe megadrought in recorded history.[18] The experts of the GSL Strike Team used sophisticated hydrologic models to determine that the ongoing drought explains 15-23 percent of the water loss from GSL over the last thirty-five years.

Water Diversion

Water diverted from the tributary streams will lead to reductions in the measured streamflow. The Bear, Weber, and Jordan Rivers have all experienced decreased streamflow over the last 125 years (fig. 8). The Bear River, which delivers about 50 percent of water to GSL, has seen a decline of nearly 38 percent. The Weber River, which delivers about 20 percent of water to GSL, has seen an even more dramatic streamflow decrease indicating significant depletion by natural and human systems. In contrast, the Jordan River, which delivers 25 percent of water to GSL, has seen comparatively little change. The experts of the GSL Strike Team determined that natural and human consumptive use explains 67-73 percent of the water loss from GSL over the last thirty-five years.

The Utah Division of Water Resources recently completed a thirty-year water depletion budget that shows that 67 percent of water depletions are for agricultural purposes. Municipal and industrial use depletes 18 percent, while mineral extraction depletes an additional 8 percent. Further analysis revealed that more than

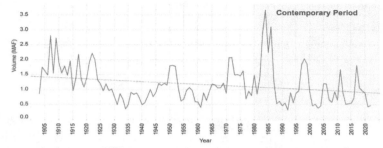

Source: Data from USGS gage 10126000 Bear river Near Corrinne with missing data (1957-1963) and values prior to 1949 derived from USGS gage 10118000 Bear River near Collinston (Analysis by David Tarboton)

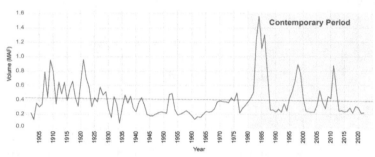

Source: Data from USGS gage 10170490 (1944-2022) with modeled data from 1902-1943 (Analysis by Margaret Wolf)

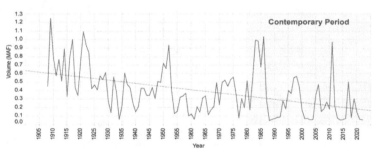

Source: Data from USGS gage 10141000 Weber River near Plain City, UT

Figure 8. Time series measurements of the average volumes of water delivered to Great Salt Lake (in units of millions of acre-feet) via the Bear River (top), Weber River (center), and Jordan River (bottom).

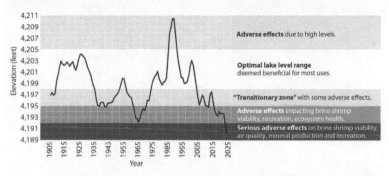

Average Annual Elevation of Great Salt Lake with Elevation Zones, 1903–2022

Sources: US Geological Survey Historical Elevation at Saltair Boat Harbor; Utah Division of Forestry, Fire and State Lands, GSL Lake Elevation Matrix, 2013

Figure 9. Great Salt Lake elevation matrix showing the optimal lake level range based on ecological health and the absence of significant adverse impacts.

half of the agricultural water depletions support the growth of alfalfa and hay.[19]

Consequences of a Shrinking Great Salt Lake

The Utah Division of Forestry, Fire, and State Lands assembled a GSL Lake Elevation Matrix (fig. 9) that established an optimal lake level range based on ecological health and the absence of significant adverse impacts.[20] As the lake deviates from the optimal range (either upward or downward), undesirable impacts ensue. Low lake levels have already surpassed tipping points for dust production and loss of recreation. During the fall of 2022 when the lake reached its historical low, the lake came dangerously close to both the industrial and salinity tipping points. Each of these tipping points has economic, ecological, and human health implications.

Threats to Human Health

Dust plumes from the GSL playa were observed in Salt Lake City as early as 2010, indicating that the dust production tipping point was reached more than a decade ago. These dust plumes can reduce

Figure 10. Example of a dust plume from Great Salt Lake impacting the air quality in downtown Salt Lake City on November 16, 2016. These images were captured from a webcam mounted on the roof of the William Browning Building on the University of Utah campus looking west. Great Salt Lake is on the right side of the image and the wind was blowing from the north (i.e., right to left) after the passage of a cold front. The images were captured at 15:17:40 MDT (A), 15:48:00 MDT (B), and 16:20:18 MDT (C), respectively. [Photos courtesy of the Department of Atmospheric Sciences, University of Utah]

the horizontal visibility to <1 mile (fig. 10) and temporarily increase the mass concentrations of particulate matter (PM) above the National Ambient Air Quality Standards (NAAQS) established by the U.S. Environmental Protection Agency (EPA) to protect human health.[21] Dust storms are most likely to occur during spring and fall when strong cold fronts pass through the area, but can also be triggered by the outflow from summertime thunderstorms.[22]

Exposure to PM can cause short-term health effects such as eye, nose, throat, and lung irritation, coughing, sneezing, runny nose, and shortness of breath.[23] It can also adversely affect lung function and worsen medical conditions such as asthma and heart disease. Scientific studies have linked increases in daily PM exposure with increased respiratory and cardiovascular hospital admissions, emergency department visits, and deaths.[24] Long-term exposure to PM is also associated with increased rates of chronic bronchitis, reduced lung function, and increased mortality from lung cancer, heart disease, stroke, and diabetes. Children, the elderly, and those with preexisting respiratory conditions such as asthma and chronic obstructive pulmonary disease (COPD) are the most susceptible to adverse health impacts from exposure to PM, but everyone can be affected if the concentrations exceed the NAAQS.

In addition to PM, the dust also contains potentially harmful elements such as aluminum, antimony, arsenic, chlorine, cobalt, copper, iron, lanthanum, lithium, manganese, uranium, vanadium, and zirconium at levels that exceed the Regional Screening Levels (RSLs) established by the EPA.[25] Chronic exposure to these elements over a long period can result in a wide variety of adverse health impacts including, but not limited to, an increased cancer risk. However, determining the risk posed by these contaminants of potential concern will require further research to ascertain the actual exposure frequency and atmospheric concentrations. Although the dust likely contains a wide range of bacteria and fungi, research into identifying the endemic species has only just begun. Thus, the potential health impacts of biologic components in the dust are currently unknown.

Snowpack Reduction

A shrinking GSL can lead to both a reduction in the amount of snow in the adjacent Wasatch Mountains and an increase in the melt rate due to the deposition of dust that darkens the surface.[26] Lake-effect snow is a weather phenomenon that occurs when cold air moves over a warmer body of water where it picks up both moisture and heat.[27] This destabilizes the air mass, which causes the warm moist air to rise, where it cools and eventually forms snow. The amount of snowfall can be significant, particularly in areas downwind of a water body where the cold air mass carrying the moisture and heat makes landfall, and in downwind mountainous areas where the air mass is forced upward by the topography. Scientists have estimated that the presence of GSL increases the snowpack in the adjacent Wasatch Mountains by 5-8 percent. This amount may not sound significant, but much of the lake-effect snow falls in October and November, which provides a much-needed base for ski areas and reduces the need for costly artificial snow generation. As GSL shrinks, it becomes less efficient at transferring heat and moisture to the atmosphere. As a result, lake-effect snow production will decrease as the surface area of the lake decreases and the salinity increases.

Blowing dust is transported away from the playa by the same strong winds that generated it in the first place. The particles with aerodynamic diameters > 10 micrometers (μm) will be removed from the atmosphere by gravitational settling within a few hours. The coarse-mode particles with aerodynamic diameters between 10 and 2.5 μm will remain in the atmosphere for a day or so. The fine-mode particles with aerodynamic diameters < 2.5 μm (i.e., $PM_{2.5}$) will remain in the atmosphere for up to two weeks because the only way to remove these particles is via precipitation rainout/washout.[28] Whether through gravitational settling or precipitation rainout/washout, large quantities of dust can be deposited to the snow in the adjacent mountains during a dust transport event.

When dust is deposited to the snowpack, it makes the surface darker and less reflective than clean snow. The darker surface absorbs more solar radiation which in turn accelerates the rate at which the snow melts. Scientists have studied this effect and have determined that dust deposition in the Wasatch Mountains can cause the snowpack to melt two to three weeks sooner than during clean (non-dust) conditions.[29] The accelerated snowmelt due to dust can exacerbate flooding and reduce groundwater recharge.

Loss of Recreation Opportunities

Boating

GSL has a long sailing history that dates back to the mid-1800s. Several sailing clubs, including the Great Salt Lake Yacht Club (established in 1877), were formed during the nineteenth century. These clubs organized races and regattas on the lake that drew large crowds of spectators from nearby communities. To support the boating community, the state of Utah built two public marinas: one on the southern shore of the lake near Saltair and a smaller one on the northern tip of Antelope Island. There are also a couple of privately owned and operated marinas that serve the brine shrimp industry. As the lake elevation drops, water-based activities become more challenging as boat ramps and marinas are left high and dry. The marina on the northern tip of Antelope Island became unusable as early as 2014, signifying that the recreation tipping point was near. In 2017, the state of Utah spent $1.3 million to dredge the entrance to the marina on the southern shore in an attempt to keep the waters navigable. Unfortunately, the historically low water levels of 2022 forced the removal of the last remaining boats from the marina on the southern shore.[30] The closure of the last public marina indicated that the recreation tipping point had been reached and that the once-thriving boating community will be forced to endure a hiatus of uncertain duration.

Birding and Bird Habitats

GSL and its surrounding wetlands provide birdwatchers with a unique opportunity to view a wide variety of bird species, including several that are rare or endangered. As the lake elevation decreases, the availability of wetland habitats for birds will be greatly reduced, leading to changes in bird populations and distributions.[31] The shrinking lake also results in the loss of important nesting and feeding areas for several species of shorebirds, including American Avocets, Black-necked Stilts, and Wilson's Phalaropes. These birds rely on shallow wetlands around the lake for nesting and feeding, and their populations can be greatly impacted by changes in water levels. The American White Pelican is an iconic species that has also been heavily impacted by the shrinking lake. Pelicans prefer to nest on remote islands and beaches around the lake, including a large colony on Gunnison Island. The Utah Division of Wildlife Resources estimated that the island once hosted 20,000 breeding pairs. Unfortunately, lake elevation decreases exposed a land bridge, which allowed predators easy access to the island. As a result, the number of breeding pelican pairs on Gunnison Island has plummeted.

Waterfowl Hunting

Waterfowl hunting is another popular activity that is also being impacted by the shrinking GSL. As the lake recedes, the quality of wetland habitat for waterfowl is reduced, which can impact the number and diversity of waterfowl species that are available for hunting. The reduction in wetland habitat may create increased competition among hunters for the remaining hunting sites, potentially leading to overcrowding and conflicts. The shrinking GSL can also impact the timing of waterfowl migration and the availability of food resources. Some species of waterfowl may alter their migration patterns or change their feeding behaviors in response to changes in the lake ecosystem, which can make them more difficult for hunters to locate and harvest.

Swimming

Swimming in GSL has a long and storied history, dating back to the early days of the settlement of the region. In the late 1800s and early 1900s, GSL was a popular destination for tourists seeking to experience the unique landscape and mineral-rich waters of the lake. In the 1920s and 1930s, the lake was home to several swimming clubs and competitions, including the annual Salt Lake Marathon Swim, which attracted swimmers from across the country.[32] Various swim competitions have continued sporadically through the years, but safety concerns related to the lake's changing shoreline (due to low water levels) and the increasing industrialization of the surrounding area have reduced their popularity. Taking a swim in GSL these days is still popular with tourists but requires forethought and planning, as it can be quite a distance to reach the water and even farther for the water to get deep enough for floating.

Economic Loss

The brine shrimp and mineral extraction industries, which contribute more than $1.3 billion annually to the economy of Utah, are both threatened by the receding lake. Brine shrimp cysts that are harvested during the winter are important in aquaculture because they are a valuable source of high quality, nutritious food for a variety of aquatic organisms including fish and crustaceans. Cysts are small, hard-shelled structures that contain a dormant brine shrimp embryo. They are produced by female brine shrimp as a means of surviving unfavorable environmental conditions such as high salinity, low food availability, or changes in water temperature. GSL provides approximately 45 percent of the world's supply of brine shrimp cysts and generates annual revenue in excess of $67 million. GSL brine shrimp (*Artemia franciscana*) can tolerate high levels of salt due to several unique adaptations, including the ability to selectively absorb and excrete ions and other molecules, as well as the ability to regulate the concentration of salts and other solutes within their cells.[33] These adaptations allow them to maintain the proper balance of water and ions within their bodies for salinity levels ranging from 12–16 percent. When water evaporates from the lake it leaves the salt behind, which causes the salinity levels to increase. In November 2022, the salinity of the southern arm of GSL reached 19 percent, well beyond the optimal range for the brine shrimp. These high salt levels severely stress the brine shrimp and can eventually lead to dehydration, cellular damage, and death. Consequently, the future of the brine shrimp industry is dependent on returning the salinity of the lake to optimal levels.

The mineral extraction industry, which produces valuable products such as potash, magnesium, lithium, and road salt, transports water to large evaporation pools via a series of canals that extend into the lake. As the lake elevation decreases, the canals must be deepened and extended at great cost to maintain access to water from GSL. U.S. Magnesium, which operates on the western side of the southern arm of GSL, is the sole producer of magnesium metal in the United States. Magnesium is used in a variety of industrial and commercial applications, including the production of aluminum and other metals, as a component of fertilizers and animal feed, and as a component of some medications and supplements.[34] As the lake neared its historical low in late 2022, the U.S. Magnesium canals were barely functional. A dredging permit application was submitted to the state but it was not approved due to environmental concerns. Thus, U.S. Magnesium (and other extraction companies) will lose access to GSL water and be forced to cease production if the lake continues its downward trend. Such a scenario would result in a loss of more than $1 billion annually to the economy of Utah.

Ecosystem Collapse

The GSL food web is relatively simple compared to most ecosystems because of the extreme harshness of the hypersaline environment.[35] At the base of the food web are green algae (*Dunaliella virdis*) and blue-green algae (*Cochochloris*). These primary producers use raw materials such as nitrogen and carbon dioxide to harvest energy from the sun. Brine shrimp and brine flies are primary consumers that get energy from eating producers such as algae. Higher up the food web are the millions of birds that consume the brine shrimp and brine flies.

The salinity of GSL is related to the volume of water in the lake, which is itself related to lake elevation. When water evaporates, the volume and lake level decrease while the amount of dissolved salts remains the same. The concentration of salts in the remaining water then increases, resulting in an increased salinity. The salinity of the southern arm of the lake, where all of the tributary streams enter GSL, varies considerably on seasonal and annual bases but has averaged about 12.8 percent over the last thirty-five years.[36] The northern arm of the lake, which is bounded on the south by an earthen railroad causeway, has had an average salinity of 25.2 percent over the same time period. For comparison purposes, seawater has an average salinity between 3.2–3.6 percent.[37] The salinity in the northern arm is so high that neither *Dunaliella virdis* nor *Cochochloris* can survive. In fact, the only algae that can thrive in the northern arm is *Dunaliella salina*. This extremophile, which has high concentrations of β-carotene to protect it against intense sunlight, gives the GSL's northern arm its distinctive pink coloration.[38]

Although brine shrimp and brine flies can both tolerate high salinity, even they have limits. For example, the optimal salinity range for brine shrimp is 12–16 percent. At salinities above this range, brine shrimp become stressed and spend much of their energy shedding salt (osmoregulation). As a result, they grow slower and have lower reproductive rates. The salt tolerance of brine flies is much less studied. However, as the lake elevation decreases it exposes microbialite communities to the atmosphere, where they quickly die. Microbialites are structures that are formed by colonies of microorganisms such as bacteria and algae. At GSL, microbialites form mounds (biomineralization). The microbialite mounds are similar to coral reefs in the ocean because they are living rock structures that provide both food and habitat.[39] Brine fly larvae, for example, feed extensively on the microorganisms that make up microbialites. As the lake shrinks and salinity increases, a tipping point will eventually be reached where the brine shrimp and brine flies disappear from the ecosystem. If this occurs, the food web will be broken and the millions of birds that utilize GSL will suffer catastrophically due to a lack of food. The salinity tipping point is likely around a salinity level of 19-20 percent. During the late summer and early fall of 2022, the salinity increased to 19 percent and brine fly populations began to plummet, indicating that the ecosystem was on the verge of collapse.

What Do We Know about Dust from Great Salt Lake?

Although there are many consequences of a shrinking GSL, the one most likely to adversely impact the greatest number of people is blowing dust. Dust plumes have been blowing off the lake since at least 2010. These plumes increase the concentrations of both PM_{10} and $PM_{2.5}$ particles, reduce horizontal visibility, and deposit a layer of dust on the surrounding communities and adjacent mountains. This section will address the following three questions:

- Where does the dust originate?
- Does the dust pose a threat to human health?
- What is the best way to mitigate the dust?

To answer these questions, I will summarize the results of the Great Salt Lake Dust Plume Study that I conducted between 2016 and 2018.

Where Does the Dust Originate?

Dust emission from land surfaces is variable in both space and time because it requires a specific combination of physical and meteorological conditions.[40] Physical characteristics that promote dust emission include a high fraction of fine particles (i.e., silt and clay), little or no vegetation, and the absence of a protective surface crust.

Meteorological conditions that promote dust emission include strong and/or gusty winds and dry soil.

Anyone who has ever grabbed a handful of sand at the beach and thrown it into the air has observed that the sand grains fall back to the ground quickly due to gravity. The situation is very different if you grab a handful of soil from a farmer's field and toss it into the air. The large clods quickly fall back to the ground, but a cloud of particles remains suspended in the atmosphere, gradually moving downwind in the form of a dust plume. The difference between these situations is the amount of fine particles in the soil. The gravitational fall speed of the PM_{10} and $PM_{2.5}$ particles is so small that their vertical velocity is controlled by random atmospheric turbulence rather than gravity. As a result, they can remain suspended in the atmosphere for periods ranging from a few hours to more than two weeks.

The presence of vegetation on the lakebed suppresses dust production by stabilizing the soil and reducing the velocity of the wind near the surface through increased friction. Physical crusts suppress dust emission by cementing the particles together and shielding the underlying soil from the wind.[41] An intact physical crust, regardless of thickness, drastically reduces the potential dust emission from a surface. Thus, dust erosion can only occur at locations where the surface crust is nonexistent or has started to erode naturally or by human disturbance.

The emission of dust from GSL is seasonal. The peak dust emission coincides with the passage of cold fronts, which are most common during the spring and fall. Dust is rarely observed during the winter because the soil is generally too wet (fig. 11). A secondary peak sometimes occurs during the summer monsoon when thunderstorms are present. Dust devils, which are common during the hottest and driest parts of the summer, can also loft dust from the surface.

A dust "hot spot" is an area where dust is emitted from the playa when the soil is dry and the winds are strong (fig. 12). These hot spots require the presence of fine soil, an erodible or non-existent

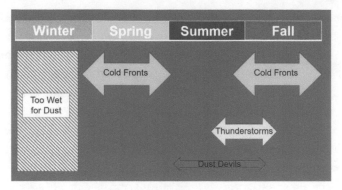

Figure 11. Seasonality of Great Salt Lake dust emissions.

crust, and little or no vegetation. On average, the GSL lakebed soil samples have a very low fine soil content (fig. 13). This means that the GSL playa is primarily composed of various size fractions of sand and is, therefore, less prone to wind erosion than many other regional dust sources. The median silt and clay fraction of 3.8 percent indicates that 50 percent of the soil samples are composed of more than 96.2 percent sand. There are, however, several areas of the lakebed with ample fine material available for dust generation. The highest silt and clay percentages exist on the eastern side of Farmington Bay (SE quadrant of the lake), in Bear River Bay (NE quadrant of the lake), and in Ogden Bay (E side of the lake). Since the primary delivery mechanism of fine soil to GSL is from the tributary streams, it is not surprising that all of these areas are near the mouths of rivers. The extreme NW quadrant of the lake also has an area with a high percentage of fine soil. This arid area does not currently support a perennial stream, but it most likely did at some point in the distant past when the climate was somewhat wetter.

Vegetation currently covers about 15 percent of the GSL playa (fig. 14). However, variation between different areas of the lakebed is quite large. The eastern side of GSL (i.e., Bear River Bay, Ogden Bay, and Farmington Bay) have the greatest amount of vegetation. There is a moderately strong correlation between the amount of vegetative cover and the fraction of fine particles in the soil,

Figure 12. Pictures of dust "hot spots" on the Great Salt Lake playa. Individual dust "hot spot" (top). Image showing how thin the protective crust can be (center). A dust "hot spot" area where smaller "hot spots" have grown and merged (bottom). [Photos by Kevin Perry]

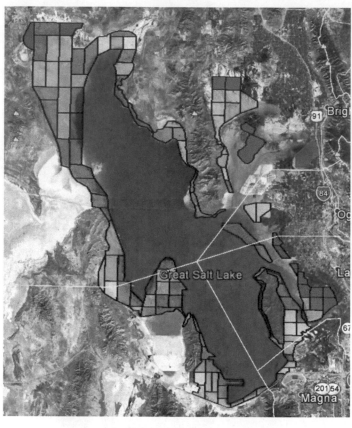

Percent Silt & Clay

<1%   1-2%   2-3%   3-4%   4-5%   5-6%   6-8%   8-10%   >10%

Figure 13. Map showing what fraction of the Great Salt Lake lakebed soil is composed of silt and clay.

indicating that vegetation struggles to survive in very sandy soils. The salt content of the soil and the length of time that an area has been exposed are likely additional controlling factors of the vegetation distributions. Because the entire lakebed was underwater as recently as 1987, all vegetation on the lakebed must be less than thirty-five years old.

Figure 14. Map showing the locations where vegetation was observed on the GSL lakebed. Red markers indicate that the vegetation occurred in areas with high concentrations of fine particles. Green markers indicate vegetation occurring in sandier soils.

Physical crusts of various thicknesses currently cover a significant fraction of the exposed lakebed of GSL (fig. 15). The surface crust survey completed in 2018 revealed that 67.6 percent of the GSL lakebed is protected by a shallow crust (i.e., < 0.5 cm). Intact thick (i.e., > 1 cm) and moderate (i.e., between 1.0 and 0.5 cm) crusts protect an additional 1.5 percent and 4.2 percent of the lakebed, respectively. The remaining 26.6 percent either has no crust or an

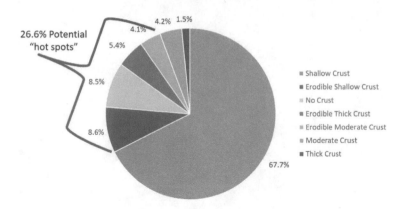

Figure 15. Summary of surface crust characteristics for the entire Great Salt Lake playa.

erodible crust of variable thickness. Farmington Bay and Bear River Bay had the highest fractions of erodible shallow crusts. Although slightly more than one-quarter of the lakebed currently has surface crust conditions conducive to dust production, some of these locations are partially vegetated or lack sufficient fine particles to produce dust. Thus, the actual percentage of the lakebed that is actively generating dust (i.e., serving as dust hot spots) was only 8.5 percent in 2018. The observed dust hot spots are congregated into four distinct clusters, one in each quadrant of the lake (fig. 16).

Does the Dust Pose a Threat to Human Health?

The EPA is authorized by the Clean Air Act[42] to establish NAAQS to protect human and ecological health by limiting the concentration of certain pollutants in outdoor air. [43] The NAAQS are based on scientific research and risk assessments that identify safe levels of exposure to each pollutant that has been causally linked to adverse health outcomes. The air pollutants currently regulated by the EPA include ozone, particulate matter (PM_{10} and $PM_{2.5}$), carbon monoxide, nitrogen oxides, sulfur dioxide, and lead. The EPA establishes both primary and secondary standards for each pollutant. Primary

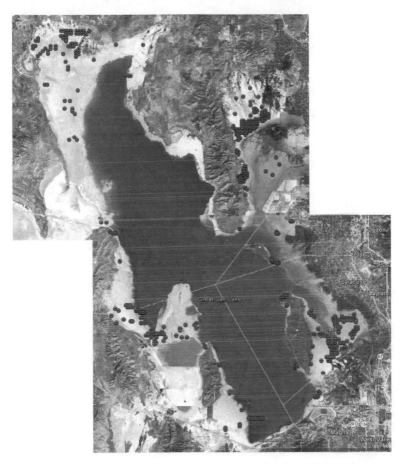

Figure 16. Map showing the location of dust "hot spots" on the Great Salt Lake playa (as of August 2018).

standards protect public health, while secondary standards protect public welfare (e.g., crops, vegetation, visibility, and animals). The 24-hour average NAAQS (primary) for PM_{10} and $PM_{2.5}$ are 150 and 35 micrograms per cubic meter ($\mu g/m^3$), respectively. Atmospheric concentrations below these thresholds are considered safe, while concentrations above these thresholds are considered unhealthy. To determine whether GSL dust poses a threat to human health due to PM_{10} and $PM_{2.5}$ exposures, the atmospheric concentrations of these pollutants must be measured during dust events.

There are hundreds of toxic air pollutants that lack the scientific research needed to establish primary safety standards. For these air toxics, the EPA requires businesses to monitor their annual emissions and report them to the Toxics Release Inventory (TRI) database.[44] The public health risk associated with air toxics depends on the dose received by individuals, the exposure pathway (ingestion, inhalation, or dermal contact), and the inherent toxicity. The toxicity and exposure pathway are relatively straightforward to determine. Dose, which is the concentration times the duration of exposure, is extremely difficult to quantify because it depends on where a person resides, their travel patterns, how much time they spend outdoors, and their respiration rate. Consequently, exposure assessments (dose measurements) are typically time consuming and expensive and are only performed when warranted.

Regional Screening Levels (RSLs) for a large number of air toxics were established by the EPA to determine whether a site-specific exposure assessment is necessary.[45] The RSLs use conservative estimates for exposure frequency and duration to identify the ambient concentrations that result in a target cancer risk of one in one million. Multiple RSLs exist for a given site depending on the degree of exposure (resident or industrial) and the exposure pathway (ingestion, inhalation, or dermal contact). Species that do not exceed the RSLs established by the EPA should not pose a health risk to the nearby residents. Species with concentrations greater than the RSLs established by the EPA have the potential to adversely impact human health and should undergo a site-specific exposure assessment to determine the actual risk levels. We refer to these species as contaminants of potential concern.

Dust plumes that come off the GSL playa occasionally raise the PM_{10} and $PM_{2.5}$ concentrations to unhealthy levels for short periods of time (i.e., several hours). However, since the NAAQS for PM is a 24-hour average, the dust plumes do not typically result in an official exceedance. Regardless, this type of acute exposure can still cause irritation of the eyes, nose, and throat, as well as respiratory symptoms such as coughing, wheezing, and shortness of breath. For people with pre-existing respiratory or cardiovascular conditions like asthma or heart disease, exposure to high levels of PM can exacerbate symptoms and lead to heart attacks or strokes.

A comprehensive soil survey of all 800 mi.^{2} of the exposed lakebed was conducted between 2016 and 2018 to determine whether there are potentially dangerous levels of toxic species in the dust originating from the GSL playa. This study identified thirteen contaminants of potential concern that exceeded the industrial or residential RSLs established by the EPA. These contaminants included aluminum, antimony, arsenic, chlorine, cobalt, copper, iron, lanthanum, lithium, manganese, uranium, vanadium, and zirconium. Of these elements, the most concerning was arsenic because every soil measurement exceeded the industrial RSL by more than an order of magnitude (i.e., > a factor of 10). Chronic exposure to arsenic-laden dust over an extended period of time (a decade or longer) has the potential to increase the rates of lung cancer, skin cancer, and bladder cancer in populations living downwind of the exposed playa.

The storms that are most likely to generate dust plumes on the GSL playa typically involve 12-18 hours of strong pre-frontal winds from the south (SW to SE) followed by the passage of a cold front and three to six hours of strong post-frontal winds from the northwest (W to N). Thus, all 2.5 million Wasatch Front residents are downwind of the lake during some part of a storm passage (fig. 17). The cold fronts can pass with or without precipitation. A dry cold front will generate a well-defined dust plume that moves from the GSL playa into the surrounding communities. Raindrops associated with a wet cold front can remove particles via rainout and washout. Rainout occurs when cloud droplets form directly on dust particles. Washout occurs when falling raindrops collect dust particles as they fall from the sky. Both of these mechanisms remove PM from the atmosphere and deposit it on the surface, and when the rain stops, almost everything is coated in a very noticeable layer of dust. Because wet cold fronts actively remove PM from the atmosphere,

Figure 17. Image showing the range of directions dust plumes can be blown from each of the dust "hot spot" regions of the Great Salt Lake playa.

dry cold fronts tend to have higher PM_{10} and $PM_{2.5}$ concentrations. As a result, dry cold fronts are more likely to generate PM_{10} and $PM_{2.5}$ concentrations that exceed the NAAQS and pose an acute health risk.

What is the Best Way to Mitigate GSL Dust?

The unequivocal best way to reduce dust emissions from the GSL playa is to return water to the lake and cover the dust hot spots with water. Actions to reduce dust emissions without water are extremely expensive and oftentimes ineffective. Owens (Dry) Lake in California served as a testbed for dust mitigation strategies that started in the 1980s and continue through the present day. The City of Los Angeles first diverted water from the Owens River in 1913, and by 1926 Owens Lake was dry. Over time, Owens (Dry) Lake became the worst dust source in North America, routinely inundating the surrounding communities with massive plumes of dust laden with silica and arsenic.[46] Due to frequent violations of the NAAQS for PM_{10}, the federal government forced the Los Angeles Department of Power and Water to develop a dust mitigation strategy. They tried a wide variety of dust mitigation techniques including wind fences, tillage, vegetation management using drip irrigation, chemical dust suppressants, and gravel. After spending more than $2.5 billion on dust mitigation efforts, they concluded that the most cost-effective dust suppression technique was to level the playa and flood it with a few inches of water.[47]

Using dust mitigation techniques for GSL other than returning water to the lake would be prohibitively expensive. The Owens (Dry) Lake playa is approximately 110 mi.[2] while the exposed playa of GSL exceeds 800 mi.[2] In addition, much of the GSL playa is incapable of supporting the heavy equipment needed to implement non-water mitigation techniques. Managed vegetation is also not an option because of the saltiness of the soil and the periodic flooding of the playa that occurs during winter.

The elevation of every dust hot spot identified during the GSL soil survey completed in 2018 was determined using a digital elevation model (DEM) generated using airborne lidar.[48] The DEM was used to determine the relationship between the lake elevation and the fraction of dust hot spots covered by water (fig. 18). It is estimated that 50 percent of the dust hot spots are at elevations less than 4197.6 ft. above mean sea level. Thus, if the lake were to rise to this level, half of the known dust sources would be underwater. The lake would need to rise to 4202.2 ft. to cover up 80 percent of the dust hot spots. This represents a lake level increase of 13.5 ft. above the historical lake level minimum of 4188.7 ft. observed in November 2022. Unfortunately, the dust tipping point was the first one to topple and will be the last to be redressed as lake levels rise in the future.

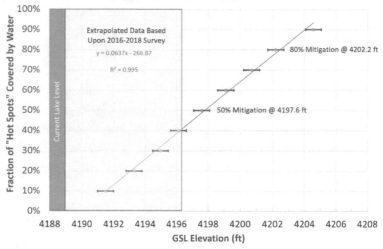

Figure 18. Elevation distribution of all dust "hot spots" identified on the Great Salt Lake playa. This figure shows what fraction of dust "hot spots" will be covered by water at various lake elevations. Data below a lake elevation of 4196 ft is extrapolated because the lake elevation was at 4195 ft when the soil survey was completed in 2018.

CAN GREAT SALT LAKE BE SAVED?

I am cautiously optimistic about the future of GSL because the solutions are within our control and the citizens of Utah and their leaders are committed to saving the lake. Unlike the Colorado River Watershed, which has been decimated by climate change and the ongoing megadrought, the shrinkage of GSL is predominately the result of unsustainably large water diversions from the tributary streams that feed the lake. A study completed by scientists at Utah State University determined that Utahns divert 30 percent too much water each year from the Bear, Weber, and Jordan Rivers.[49] If we reduce our water diversions by this amount, GSL will return to a state where lake levels will decrease when the snowpack is below normal and increase when the snowpack is above normal. As of 2023, water diversions are so enormous that the breakeven point for the lake is a snowpack of 130 percent of normal. This situation is clearly unsustainable and explains why the lake level has been decreasing so rapidly over the last few decades. To achieve this 30 percent conservation goal, we must partner with and invest in agriculture.

Several reports have devised strategies to replenish the lake. These include the Great Salt Lake Advisory Council Report (2020),[50] the Great Salt Lake Resolution (HCR-10) Steering Group Report (2020),[51] and the Great Salt Lake Strike Team Policy Assessment (2023). Many of the strategies outlined in these reports have already been implemented, but much work remains. However, I am confident that as long as the people of Utah remain committed to saving GSL, the Utah State Legislature will continue to provide leadership and funding to enact meaningful changes to save the incredible ecological oasis known as Great Salt Lake.

NOTES

1. Utah Division of Wildlife Resources, "Birds: An Avian Oasis," Great Salt Lake Ecosystem Program, https://wildlife.utah.gov/gslep/wildlife/birds.html.

2. Bioeconomics Inc. *Economic Significance of the Great Salt Lake to the State of Utah*, Salt Lake City, UT: Great Salt Lake Advisory Council, January 2012, https://documents.deq.utah.gov/water-quality/standards-technical-services/great-salt-lake-advisory-council/Activities/DWQ-2012-006864.pdf.

3. ECONorthwest, *Assessment of Potential Costs of Declining Water Levels in Great Salt Lake*, Salt Lake City, UT: Great Salt Lake Advisory Council, November 2019, https://documents.deq.utah.gov/water-quality/standards-technical-services/great-salt-lake-advisory-council/activities/DWQ-2019-012913.pdf.

4. Kristen N. Yeager, William J. Steenburgh, and Trevor I. Alcott, "Contributions of Lake-Effect Periods to the Cool-Season Hydroclimate of the Great Salt Lake Basin," *Journal of Applied Meteorology and Climatology* 52, no. 2 (February 1, 2013): 341–62, https://doi.org/https://doi.org/10.1175/JAMC-D-12-077.1.

5. Beth Lopez, "Save Our Winters," *Utah Business*, April 19, 2019, https://www.utahbusiness.com/greatest-snow-on-earth/.

6. Nancy D. McCormick and John S. McCormick, *Saltair* (Salt Lake City: University of Utah Press, 1985).

7. Anastasia Hufham, "'Like a Polaroid Developed:' Ancient Footprints Found in Utah Offer Window into Human Life 12,000 Years Ago," *Salt Lake Tribune*, August 13, 2022, https://www.sltrib.com/news/2022/08/13/like-polaroid-developed-ancient/.

8. Casey P. Griffiths, Mary J. Woodger, and Susan E. Black, "The Myth About Brigham Young's 'This Is the Place' Quote," *LDS Living*, July 24, 2017, https://www.ldsliving.com/the-myth-about-brigham-youngs-this-is-the-place-quote/s/85936.

9. W. Lawrence Gates, "Modeling the Ice-Age Climate," *ACM SIGSIM Simulation Digest* 7, no. 3 (April 1976): 66–72, https://doi.org/https://doi.org/10.1145/1102746.1102757.

10. J. Wallace Gwynn, "Commonly Asked Questions about Utah's Great Salt Lake & Lake Bonneville," *Popular Geology*, 1996, https://geology.utah.gov/popular/great-salt-lake/commonly-asked-questions/.

11. Utah Geological Survey, "Ice Ages," *Popular Geology*, accessed May 9, 2023, https://geology.utah.gov/popular/ice-age/.

12. Harold E. Malde, "The Catastrophic Late Pleistocene Bonneville Flood in the Snake River Plain, Idaho," *USGS* 569 (1968).

13. U.S. Geological Survey Utah Water Science Center, "Current Conditions," Great Salt Lake Hydro Mapper, https://webapps.usgs.gov/gsl/data.html.

14. Great Salt Lake Strike Team, *Great Salt Lake Policy Assessment: A Synthesized Resource Document for the 2023 General Legislative Session*, Kem C. Gardner Policy Institute University of Utah, February 9, 2023, https://gardner.utah.edu/wp-content/uploads/GSL-Assessment-Feb2023.pdf?x71849.

15. Kevin E. Trenberth, "Changes in Precipitation with Climate Change," *Climate Research* 47, no. 1 (2011): 123–38, https://doi.org/10.3354/cr00953.

16. USGCRP, *Climate Science Special Report: Fourth National Climate Assessment*, vol. 1, ed. Wuebbles, D.J., D.W. Fahey, K.A. Hibbard, D.J. Dokken, B.C. Stewart, and T.K. Maycock, U.S. Global Change Research Program, 2017.

17. Paul D. Brooks, et al., "Groundwater-Mediated Memory of Past Climate Controls Water Yield in Snowmelt-Dominated Catchments," *Water Resources Research* 57, no. 10 (September 27, 2021), https://doi.org/10.1029/2021wr030605.

18. A. Park Williams, Benjamin I. Cook, and Jason E. Smerdon, "Rapid Intensification of the Emerging Southwestern North American Mega-drought in 2020–2021," *Nature Climate Change* 12 (February 14, 2022): 232–34, https://doi.org/https://doi.org/10.1038/s41558-022-01290-z.

19. Utah Division of Water Resources, *Water Resources Plan*, December 2021, https://water.utah.gov/wp-content/uploads/2022/01/Water-Resources-Plan-Single-Page-Layout.pdf.

20. U.S. Geological Survey Utah Water Science Center, "Lake Characteristics Matrix," Great Salt Lake Hydro Mapper, May 9, 2023, https://webapps. usgs.gov/gsl/#salinity.

21. Maura Hahnenberger and Kathleen Nicoll, "Meteorological Characteristics of Dust Storm Events in the Eastern Great Basin of Utah, U.S.A," *Atmospheric Environment* 60 (December 2012): 601–12, https://doi. org/10.1016/j.atmosenv.2012.06.029.

22. W. James Steenburgh, Jeffrey D. Massey, and Thomas H. Painter, "Episodic Dust Events of Utah's Wasatch Front and Adjoining Region," *Journal of Applied Meteorology and Climatology* 51, no. 9 (2012): 1654–69, https://doi.org/10.1175/jamc-d-12-07.1.

23. Douglas W. Dockery, "Health Effects of Particulate Air Pollution," *Annals of Epidemiology* 19, no. 4 (April 2009): 257–63, https://doi.org/10.1016/j. annepidem.2009.01.018.

24. C. Ardon Pope III, David V. Bates, and Mark E. Raizenne, "Health Effects of Particulate Air Pollution: Time for Reassessment?," *Environmental Health Perspectives* 103, no. 5 (1995): 472–80, https://doi.org/10.1289/ ehp.95103472.

25. Kevin D. Perry, Erik T. Crosman, and Sebastian W. Hoch, *Results of the Great Salt Lake Plume Study (2016-2018)*, Utah Department of Natural Resources, April 2019, https://d1bbnjcim4wtri.cloudfront.net/wp-content/uploads/2019/12/10101816/GSL_Dust_Plumes_Final_Report_Complete_Document.pdf.

26. S. McKenzie Skiles et al., "Radiative Forcing by Light-Absorbing Particles in Snow," *Nature Climate Change* 8, no. 11 (2018): 964–71, https://doi. org/10.1038/s41558-018-0296-5.

27. National Weather Service, "What is a Lake Effect Snow?" accessed May 10, 2023, https://www.weather.gov/safety/winter-lake-effect-snow.

28. Henning Rodhe and Jan Grandell, "On the Removal Time of Aerosol Particles from the Atmosphere by Precipitation Scavenging," *Tellus* 24, no. 5 (1972): 442–54, https://doi.org/10.1111/j.2153-3490.1972.tb01571.x.

29. S. McKenzie Skiles and Thomas H. Painter, "Toward Understanding Direct Absorption and Grain Size Feedbacks by Dust Radiative Forcing in Snow with Coupled Snow Physical and Radiative Transfer Modeling," *Water Resources Research* 55, no. 8 (2019): 7362–78, https://doi. org/10.1029/2018wr024573.

30. Ben Winslow, "Last Boats Pulled from the Great Salt Lake Marina," *Salt Lake Tribune*, August 4, 2022, https://www.sltrib.com/news/2022/08/04/ last-boats-pulled-great-salt/.

31. Utah Division of Wildlife Resources, "Drought and the Great Salt Lake," Great Salt Lake Ecosystem Program, December 19, 2022, https://wildlife. utah.gov/gslep/about/drought.html.

32. Lynn Arave, "Lynn Arave: Back When Marathon Swimming Races Flourished in the Great Salt Lake," *Deseret News*, June 24, 2019, https://

www.deseret.com/2019/6/24/20676208/
lynn-arave-back-when-marathon-swimming-races-flourished-in-the-
great-salt-lake.

33.   Gilbert van Stappen, "Chapter 4: Artemia," in *Manual on the Production
      and Use of Live Food for Aquaculture*, ed. Patrick Lavens and Patrick
      Sorgeloos (Food and Agriculture Organization of the United Nations,
      1996).

34.   S. V. Satya Prasad et al., "The Role and Significance of Magnesium in
      Modern Day Research—A Review," *Journal of Magnesium and Alloys* 10,
      no. 1 (2022): 1-61, https://doi.org/10.1016/j.jma.2021.05.012.

35.   Genetic Science Learning Center University of Utah, "Great Salt Lake
      Food Web," Extreme Environments: Great Salt Lake, accessed May 10,
      2023, https://learn.genetics.utah.edu/content/gsl/foodweb/.

36.   Madeline F. Merck and David G. Tarboton, "The Salinity of the Great Salt
      Lake and Its Deep Brine Layer," *Water* 15, no. 8 (2023): 1488, https://doi.
      org/10.3390/w15081488.

37.   U.S. Geological Survey, "Why Is the Ocean Salty?" Frequently Asked
      Questions: Ocean, accessed May 10, 2023, https://www.usgs.gov/faqs/
      why-ocean-salty.

38.   Aharon Oren, "The Ecology of Dunaliella in High-Salt Environments,"
      Journal of Biological Research-Thessaloniki 21, no. 1 (2014), https://doi.
      org/10.1186/s40709-014-0023-y.

39.   Melody R. Lindsay, Eric C. Dunham, and Eric S. Boyd, "Microbialites of
      Great Salt Lake," in *Great Salt Lake Biology*, ed. Bonnie Baxter and Jamie
      Butler (Springer, Cham, 2020), 87–118, https://doi.
      org/10.1007/978-3-030-40352-2_4.

40.   Kerstin Schepanski, "Transport of Mineral Dust and Its Impact on
      Climate," *Geosciences* 8, no. 5 (2018): 151, https://doi.org/10.3390/
      geosciences8050151.

41.   Mark R. Sweeney, "Dust Emission Processes," *Treatise on Geomorphology*
      (2022): 235–58, https://doi.org/10.1016/b978-0-12-818234-5.00015-8.

42.   Clean Air Act, 42 U.S.C. §§7401 to 7671q.

43.   U.S. Environmental Protection Agency, "NAAQS Table," Criteria Air
      Pollutants, March 15, 2023, https://www.epa.gov/criteria-air-pollutants/
      naaqs-table.

44.   U.S. Environmental Protection Agency, "What Is the Toxics Release
      Inventory?" Toxics Release Inventory (TRI) Program, January 25, 2023,
      https://www.epa.gov/toxics-release-inventory-tri-program/
      what-toxics-release-inventory.

45.   U.S. Environmental Protection Agency, "Regional Screening Levels
      (RSLs)," Risk Assessment, November 18, 2022, https://www.epa.gov/risk/
      regional-screening-levels-rsls.

46.   Thomas A. Cahill et al., "Saltating Particles, Playa Crusts and Dust
      Aerosols at Owens (Dry) Lake, California," *Earth Surface Processes and*

Landforms 21, no. 7 (July 1996): 621–39, https://doi.org/https://doi.
org/10.1002/(SICI)1096-9837(199607)21:7<621::AID-ESP661>3.0.CO;2-E.

47. National Academies of Sciences, Engineering, and Medicine, *Effectiveness and Impacts of Dust Control Measures for Owens Lake,*Washington, DC: The National Academies Press, 2020, https://doi.org/10.17226/25658.

48. Utah Geospatial Resource Center, "2016 Great Salt Lake and Utah Lake LiDAR Elevation Data," Elevation and Terrain Data, accessed May 10, 2023, https://gis.utah.gov/data/elevation-and-terrain/2016-lidar-gsl/.

49. Wayne A. Wurtsbaugh et al., "Decline of the World's Saline Lakes," *Nature Geoscience* 10, no. 11 (2017): 816–21, https://doi.org/10.1038/ ngeo3052.

50. Steve Clyde, Emily Lewis, Bob Harding, and Jeff DenBleyker, *Water Strategies for Great Salt Lake: Legal Analysis and Review of Select Water Strategies for Great Salt Lake*, Great Salt Lake Advisory Council, September 10, 2020, https://documents.deq.utah.gov/water-quality/ standards-technical-services/great-salt-lake-advisory-council/activities/ DWQ-2020-017633.pdf.

51. Great Salt Lake Resolution (HCR-10) Steering Group, *Recommendations to Ensure Adequate Water Flows to Great Salt Lake and Its Wetlands*, December 2020, https://ffsl.utah.gov/wp-content/uploads/GSL_ HCR10Report_final_Dec2020b.pdf.

About the Author

Photo by Evan Bush.

Dr. Kevin Perry has been a professor in the Department of Atmospheric Sciences at the University of Utah since 2002. He holds a B.S. in meteorology from Iowa State University and a Ph.D. in atmospheric sciences from the University of Washington. He has participated in more than twenty air quality projects ranging from local-scale pollution events to the intercontinental transport of pollutants, and served as chair of the Department of Atmospheric Sciences from 2011 to 2018. For the last decade, Dr. Perry has focused his attention on dust plumes originating from the exposed playas in the Intermountain West, especially Great Salt Lake.